20 DAYS OF SUMMER

J.Kennedy

BookLeaf
Publishing

India | USA | UK

20 Days of Summer © 2021

J.Kennedy

Presentation by *BookLeaf Publishing*

Web: www.bookleafpub.com

E-mail: info@bookleafpub.com

ISBN: 9789358366600

First edition 2021

I.

Enlighten Me

With your words

With your touch

With your smile

Let me feel you deep within

Within my mind

Within my ocean

Caress me with your fingers

Your sense of humor

Your sense of style

Look at me like I'm your prey

Take me in and cradle me under your
wings

Enlighten me with your energy

Brighten my day with your eyes

Kiss me like it's our last moment together

Enlighten me

2.

You're beautiful

Don't listen to what others have to say

Don't let them discourage you in being
great

Don't live up to their standard of how you
should be

Live your life the way it ought to be

To benefit you

To be only justified by you

To be streamers and glitters because every
day should be about you

Don't let them tear down your ego

Or undermine your effort

You're a shining star and a legend in these
parts

Walk with your head high

Walk with meaning

Don't let anyone tell you different

You're beautiful and I mean it

3.

Try harder

It's better than not doing anything at all

Give it all your might and do what you
think is right

No one is asking you to run a marathon or
to be a hero

Just asking you to try

Not asking of anything that will hurt you
but be beneficial to you

Would never put you in harm's way, but
you not trying is detrimental to us both

I want you to succeed

Want you to be better

You can't become a mathematician over
night

You first have to try

I know it might be scary but trying is
better than doing nothing at all

4.

As the sun rises I think of you

I think of your goodness

Your aura

Your sensuality

Your heart of gold

I think about your ups and downs

Good and bad

Your lies

And the many fights we had

As the sun rises I think of us

The kisses

The cuddles

The laughter

I think about my mood swings

My distance

Anxiety and the countless times I shunned you

As the sun rises I think of me

How I can be better

My wanting to grow

To start a family I can call my own

As the sun rises

5.

You are my dream come true

Not a moment goes by when I'm not
praying for you

Praying for you to bless this Earth, my
heart, my arms

I think about you all the time; thinking of
spoiling you, holding you, and loving you
unconditionally

I wonder if I will be a good mom

Will I be fair, too friendly or
inexperienced when it comes to you?

I anticipate that you won't be easy, but I
hope I will be able to give you the
attention that you need and deserve

I wish we would have met by now. The
wait is driving me crazy

I do want to be able to provide for you, so
I'm working extremely hard

I do want to be healthy for you, so those nine months are joyous and not difficult for you or me

I want to be mentally prepared for you, so I can endure anything you may put in my way

I hope I will be perfect for you, as I know you will be for me

But until that time comes, I'll be waiting patiently

Waiting to love you for eternity

To hold you for days never end

And to share a bond that can never be broken or torn apart

But until then, I'll continue to dream of you.

6.

Touch me with your eyes

Entertain my mind with your mouth

Drive me insane with your fingers

Entice me with words

Everlasting wisdom that creeps deep
within my soul

Caress me with knowledge that will have
me open like the sea

Drown me with laughter that will have me
coming back for more

Erupting like a volcano

Leaving nothing untouched

Begging for mercy

Enduring the heavens as I look above and
into the abyss

Soothe me with your energy

Craving more and more of you everyday

Every second of every breath that I take

7.

Do you know what love is?

Have you ever experienced a feeling so
real?

Have you ever been in love that left you
speechless?

Love that makes you listen to 90s RnB?

Love that is not materialistic

Love that lingers after the breakup

Have you ever experienced a broken heart?

It feels like a heart attack

Have you ever loved someone and they
never loved you back?

Ever tried to understand someone, but all
they do is push you away?

Have you ever experienced love?

Not what social media portrays it to be

But that Old School love

That Dwayne and Whitley love

That Claire and Cliff love

That Carl Thomas Summer Rain love

8.

I'm not going to compete for your heart

It wasn't mine to begin with

Can't understand why it's hard to let go

I'm good at walking away

But somehow, I find myself stuck

Sinking

Like quicksand

Consuming me

Burying me alive

Death does not suit me

You're giving me an early grave

Starting to despise you

Looking at you is suffocating

Breathing you is burning my soul from
within

9.

Another day, another moment

A lifetime, an eternity

Every second counts

Every breath isn't wasted

I'm thankful for it all

I'm grateful for each day

10.

Think of me as you would of you

Would you be nicer?

Would you be more supportive?

Think of me as you would of the stars

Would you wish upon me?

Would stare at me endlessly?

Think of me as you would of an exotic
bird

Would you admire how beautiful I was?

Would you want to show me off?

Think of me as you would of the
strawberry moon

Would you put your faith in me for
harvest?

Think of me as you would of the
Caribbean Sea

Would you want to float within and trust me to carry you to a land of beauty?

Think of me as you would of you

Would you want the best for me as I of you?

II.

Can you hold me one more time?

Again, for the night

For that comfort

Maybe that security

I just want to feel you

Just to be reminded of how you ever made
me feel

Just to be captivated once more

To remember the reason of why I fell in
love with you

To embrace your essence

To be lost in your presence

Can you hold me one more time?

So that I can be swept away in your aura

So I can daydream about heaven

So I can be aware of my heart's beating
rhythm

12.

It's amazing how beautiful you are

You're admirable

Your lips down to your petite toes

You have a big heart

A caring and loving person

How can someone hurt you?

Who would want to?

You're smart

You've come a long way

You fight every day, not all you will win

You're determined

Dedicated

Sweet in your own way

No need to convince yourself

Yes, sometimes I know it can be hazy

Yes, I know at times it can be difficult

Know your worth

Take your time and figure it out but know

You're beautiful

13.

I want the experience

I want to try something new

I want to learn from what is taught

I want to dabble with the thought

With the thought of being me

With the thought of being free

Free to fall and get back up

Free to say that's something I'll do again

Free to be comfortable in a new
environment

I want the experience

I want to explore the skies and valley lows

I want to be able to say no I didn't like and
probably do it again

I want to be free to make my own
decisions

I want to be free to say no without the
ugly looks

I want to be free to be me

14.

I would be lying if I said I didn't love you

I could not be honest with myself if I said
I was okay being without

I would be out of my mind to ever say you
weren't good enough for me

It's been an emotional roller coaster

Scared straight not knowing the flow of
the ride

If it ever felt that I wasn't trying, that's
not true

I just put in extra work than most and it
physically drains me

Loving you was never a task; it was a
natural entity

When I love, it's more of a force that pulls
my energy to let you know that it's real

So forgive me if I seemed distant or unable
to love you

The truth it I loved you so much that I
started loving myself less

15.

I've been on my Trey Songz lately

Not sexually but emotionally

Listening to the words of truth

Wondering do you hear the songs as I do

Do you think and ask yourself, where have
I gone wrong?

I've been emotional lately, mind is not
over matter

Changes are not liberating

Craving the need of not feeling lonely

Being absent minded just so the day can
run by

Lost to space and time

Losing reality and at times going blind

I've been on my music melodies

Listening to only what my heart can relate
to and mending it with written words

Looking for an output in this
#20daywritingchallenge but the adhesive is
weaker than old glue

Just hoping and praying one day you'll be
true and feel the words like I do

16.

Stay strong they say

Walk with your head high

Be a better you

Don't cry

Do as you're told

Be a part of society

Just a few things I haven't yet achieved

Find one who can provide for you

Possibly love you

Get married

Have babies

Just a few things I can't seem to
accomplish

Save your money

Get a house

Get a good paying job

Work hard and depend on no one

Just a few things I wasn't able to get right

Stay thin

Be polite and friendly

Don't eat so much

Smile some

Just a few things I failed to acknowledge

Doing or not doing nothing ever feels
right

Loving or being loved seems to have me
feeling empty

Being a part of something doesn't feel
great

The amount of degrees don't even matter
anymore if there's no one to share the
success with or criticize you because
you're trying

17.

Some days are better than others

It's best to try and take it one at a time

Building energy just to say hi

Looking for the rainbow outside my
window

All I see is clouds of grey

Wishing for that sweet Aura

That sweet taste of a better day

But it's a sour peach

It's becoming overwhelming for me

No longer do I want to pretend but it gets
me through the seconds

Being tough for the crowd but barely
surviving for the soul

18.

Always and forever

Not a vow we made

Not the words we exchanged

But a concept that we thought would be

A trend that could last a lifetime

Along the way wires got crossed

The road is no longer the same

You see that I'm a tad bit different

More emotional than before

Am I walking away from you or at a
different pace from you?

So far that your scent is fading

Distant like the sun

Astray like a traveler from home

Always and forever

Always your woman

Sometimes those words will play with my mind

But it's a road we will meet on once again

19.

Don't pinch me, I'm dreaming

Laying here thinking about you

Watch me as I soar across the skies

Just to be closer to you

Gently touch against my skin, knowing
you truly exist

Whispers in the wind

Tears of the sun

The warmth of you nearly drains my
blood

Leaves tingles down my spine

Speechless

20.

Inner peace

Inner child

Inner thoughts

The sky is never the limit

Strive beyond what you see

Scream out loud for what you believe in

Don't let the rain ruin your plans

Continue to fight with all your might

No matter how hard or rough it will be

Don't give up

Wanting that inner peace will come

Wanting to hear your own thoughts
clearly will be

Cry if you have to

Never let go

It's not easy

Stand tall

The storm will end soon

www.ingramcontent.com/pod-product-compliance
Lightning Source LLC
LaVergne TN
LVHW051245200726
843510LV00011B/1691